The 3% Rule

The 3% Rule

The Ultimate Accountability Tool

By

Brian Oellig

Ordering Information:

Quantity sales. Special discounts are available on quantity purchases by corporations, associations, and others. Orders by U.S. trade bookstores and wholesalers. Please contact Brian Oellig via www.brianoellig.com

ISBN: 978-1-7348481-0-6

CONTENTS

DEDICATION

This book is dedicated to all the people who have moved, touched, and inspired me. I am grateful for the push in the direction of helping other people.

For the reader that holds this book in their hands, may this book be a catalyst for your expanded growth, happiness, and fulfillment.

I am humbled for the opportunity to encourage and inspire you to become the best version of yourself.

Never forget – consistent action over time will take you to where you want to be.

The 3% Rule

A Simple Question Leads to a Big Change

"Brian, if I asked you to recount your day to me," my colleague in California asked me over the phone with genuine curiosity, *"how much of it do you think you could remember right now?"*

I thought about that for five seconds and guessed, "About half?" He already had me thinking, but his follow up comment, *"Well, if you are losing roughly half of every day, or cannot recount what you did during that time, imagine expanding that out over a year."*

That really set my mind to work. "How about a lifetime?" I asked.

The question burned hot in my mind. It was easy to imagine the figure would be big enough that I determined it best to avoid that train of thought, and instead focus on what I would do from now on to ensure that I did not lose that time moving forward.

How much time would you say you lose every day?

Think about it for just a moment.

Born out of necessity to avoid despair and wasting any more time, *The 3% Rule* was born.

My Promise to You

By picking up this book, I know that you are someone that chooses to invest in themselves and wants the best for their life and everyone in their lives – family, friends, colleagues, customers, and business partners.

This investment will provide you the following if you properly apply the formula I will share with you:

Increased fulfillment, increased growth, increased happiness, and it will help you become the best version of yourself that you are meant to be.

Inside of all of us is greatness, and you are no exception.

Let's go together toward unlocking your greatness.

We Are All Human, We All Lose Track of Time

Admit it. When you read that chapter title, you nodded your head up and down. We all lose track of time. In today's world, that has never been truer. Social media & its endless notifications, advertising nearly every direction we look, and 24/7 connectivity to the world makes it difficult to remain focused, let alone conscious of our internal hourglass.

Don't forget entertainment – TV, movies, video games, and watching YouTube videos. It has never been easier for us to lose track of time in our species existence. And I predict it won't get any easier for us as we move further into the future.

"Time flies when you're having fun." That's true. How about this one?
Time flies when you're not watching it.

The problem with this is that time is the only currency that really has any true inherent value. Sure, money has value. But only because we give it value and believe that it carries value. Intrinsically, Monopoly money carries the same value as real money.

Even gold doesn't carry real inherent value. We just need a reliable measure of worth to trade with for a functioning and growing society, so we need something tangible.

We believe the green ones that look official carry value, so they do. Imagine – a world where we believed Monopoly money was the true monetary note! As a long-time fan of the game, and childhood memories of trying to win against my grandma at her house, I relish in that thought.

Let me get back on track, because we are both aware that time will continue onward whether we continue to move with it or not. I share this wonderful childhood memory as an example of how this happens – even when you don't think about it, time keeps going.

The Hourglass

The moment we are born and slapped on our little butt by the doctor, our life's hourglass is flipped over. The finite number of sand available to us begins to fall, one by one.

The reason time is hard for most people to think about is because of the fact that it runs out for us.

At this point in my life I never lose the image of the sands of time falling in the back of my mind. I have Joe Rogan and his podcast to thank for this – it was in one of his conversations where he mentioned that it is hard for him to just sit back and relax anymore. When he does it for too long, he starts to get real anxiety because he knows time is slipping away.

From the moment I heard him say that I was changed.

I gained a new awareness of time that I had not had before. Soon after that I saw the movie, "In Time," with Justin Timberlake. Please allow me to voice my frustration with how underrated this movie is, because its message is so powerful.

This movie's message is clear: It is not how much time we have left, but rather, how we use the time that we do have left. More importantly – how we use the time right now, this very minute. Because this moment is all that we have. The future and the past only exist in our minds.

In the movie the girl he pursues is disenchanted with her life, because without any meaning or value to time, life loses its meaning.

There is a scene in the movie where someone mentions how fast Justin Timberlake's character is always moving around. This is because he understands the true value of time. Even after he hits the jackpot with time, he still has difficulty slowing down.

Here I will voice some concerns I have about the future. We have seen in many instances now, Black Mirror did it well, where humanity has surpassed time by utilizing cloud-like software. This allows us to upload our digital imprint into said cloud, where we can essentially live forever.

Except, it isn't real.

The appeal is shiny, no doubt about that. Time isn't ours to manipulate or control. It exists outside and beyond us. To try to do this would be like trying to prevent the moon or sun from rising. It is law, and we do not hold the pen. I know many people on our planet suffer from chronic anxiety that is rooted in the fear of death, which is really just the top layer of the real problem - they're afraid that time runs out.

It is my intention to help people that suffer from this affliction. I believe if a perspective can be changed, a person can be changed.

Today

We often overestimate what we can do in one day, but we underestimate what we can do in ten years. The twist about this saying is that all we have is today.

By focusing on today, more specifically the activities we choose to engage in throughout the hours of the day, we gain real control over what our life looks like ten years from now.

Oftentimes we fail to begin on a new idea, project, or direction because we look so far in the future and can't imagine ever getting there. We get stuck.

The truth is – at the moment we're thinking of it, we probably can't get there right then.

But that is OK. If our desired future didn't scare us a little bit, then the future we are imagining for ourselves is not big enough. We aren't here to play in the little leagues.

Once we have a firm idea of the life and future we want to build, all we must do is give our full attention to what we're doing every day.

There is never a perfect time to begin something new and unfamiliar. All we can do is use everything we have available right now to begin building a new future. Just start.

Belief, Vision, and Desire

Belief is the rocket fuel to our why.

Whether we believe we can do it, or not, we are right. It is said so often that it is almost worn out, which is unfortunate, because it is true. If so many people parrot this phrase, why do so few truly seem to be living it?

It is like the people that say, "Another day of paradise!" to you asking how it is going.

Can we just be real for a chapter?

If we don't really believe in our heart that we can accomplish something, we probably will not accomplish that thing.

If we don't have a vision for our futures, or where we are going, then even if we have the biggest, fastest ship in the ocean, what good does it do us? None!

We need a clear vision of where we want to go and are headed, backed up by absolute conviction that we will not fail in getting to that destination someday. You have to sell yourself, before you can sell anyone on you. You have to believe in you, before anyone can bet on you. Norman Vincent Peale said it well, "You can if you think you can."

We must have an unbreakable desire to see our vision become reality.

When we combine belief with a vision that is powered by desire, we have the recipe for grand achievement.

Think about the case study of Arnold Schwarzenegger as a prime example of belief, vision, and desire in action, and what they can do for each of us:

He is born in 1947 and raised in Austria shortly after World War 2. At a young age he realizes that he does not seem to be like most of the people around him. He is not content with the future life it looks like he will have as a yodeler, or a farmer. He didn't like his environment and couldn't wait to get out of there.

Here is a key thing to know about why Arnold is the person he is – He believed he was meant for something greater and was actively thinking about it and seeking it all the time. It became the kind of obsession I've witnessed an alcoholic have, to the point they stole from a lifetime friend, just to have a drink.

You have to want it as bad as that alcoholic wanted it. OK – I'm not condoning you turn into a true to life villain. Don't go out there and start leaving people in your wake with zero regard for others.

Arnold, on the other hand, shows us what healthy (and necessary) obsession looks like by example.

His obsession for something greater, a chance to be someone greater than who he was now, was so powerful that it literally opened a door for him to get there. The seed he planted was first watered by a documentary he saw in school about America. This documentary gave him a clear goal. In America, he would be able to become what he knew inside he was meant to become.

The ray of light that began to grow this ready to germinate seed was a chance experience at a store called Bruhl. It was at this store that Arnold was introduced to a man named Reg Park.

By chance, and I say chance here, because before Arnold ran into Reg Park, he believed he could be more, do more, and become more. Reg Park's life laid the blueprint for how he could get to America. He would become Mr. Olympia, and then Mr. Universe. Little did he know it would lead to him becoming the Governor of California, marrying a Kennedy, and starring in one of the best-selling movie series ever, Terminator.

The key point here is, believe you are worthy and capable of more than you have now. Whether you are making $50,000 a year, $20,000, or one million a year – you are capable of more than you are doing now. As we grow, learn, and develop our potential also rises and expands. We can never reach "there."

This is why so many people in life have tons of cash in the bank, make millions a month even in some cases, and are still unfulfilled. It is because they don't have a clear belief and vision. They've been checking the boxes throughout their lives based upon the society they live in or the people in their lives.

Another fantastic example of the power of belief and vision is Napoleon Hill. In his chance encounter with a man that resonated with him, Andrew Carnegie, Hill found both his vision and belief from Carnegie.

It was during this conversation that Carnegie gave Hill the vision he had; Hill would visit the people of the time with exceptional financial prowess and success, and learn how they had become the people they needed to become to earn that money. During the conversation, and by asking him, Carnegie sparked a new belief that Hill did not possess before they had met.

BEWARE: Belief and Vision are the jet fuel and the road map to our best possible lives. If we do not have belief and a vision, we are doomed to mediocrity.

Don't be mediocre – we are all here to be great and do great things.

Core Values

Steve, the retired CEO of one of the two sales organizations I have gone to the battlefield every day for, had a saying that I liked -

"If you don't track it, you cannot improve it."

It is simple and accurate. Many of us march onward through life, without pausing to gauge our performance in our personal lives. In sales, the most successful salespeople hold themselves accountable for their daily activities, ability to create opportunities, advance opportunities, and close opportunities.

In manufacturing, people are held to production and quality standards.

In education, people are held to grade standards.

In sports, people are held to their championships won and records.

In life, we benefit from applying a similar philosophy to our personal lives as we do our professional lives.

Yet many of us do not hold ourselves to excellent standards. Go ahead, ask a stranger today, "What are your core values you live by?" Look in their eyes and you will see many come up with them on the fly. You will know when someone you ask has really thought their core values through, because there will be a particular energy to their response.

How does one track the "performance" metrics for our lives?

It starts with our Core Values. What are yours? If you do not have these written down somewhere that is visible to you on a daily basis, you want to take the time to do this so you too can realize the powerful benefits of having a clear set of values you will not deviate from. No, really, you need to know what you stand for, for this book and the formula to have a real, lasting, life-changing impact on you.

Without these values clearly defined, we are vulnerable to outside influences that will pull us off-course from our mission, setting us back, or worse, putting us into a hole we must dig ourselves out of.

With clearly defined core values, we have a shield to defend ourselves against dangerous influences that are aimed our way.

Once they are written down, now we can begin to consider on a daily basis, *"How well am I upholding these core values?"*

This question empowers our minds to get to work with honest feedback that we need. Without this, how can we know if the path we are on is the one we want to be on? We could very well be headed for a sudden cliff, and off we go towards the bottom. And sometimes in life, we don't get a second chance.

Beware: Without Core Values it is virtually guaranteed we will make mistakes that we will regret when faced with difficult choices. Core Values serve as our compass through the times of our life when we're faced with "The Fog of War." Make no mistake, life is a battleground, with real risks and real rewards. Sometimes, the path is not clear, but with a true compass, we can continue onward in the direction we know we should be headed.

Now, I will share with you, The 3% Rule. I do not miss the irony if I would either delay too long in sharing the rule with you, the primary reason you invested in this book, and likewise, if I made this book too long in length to read in a single sitting.

The sooner you learn it, the sooner you can use it.

IT IS SIMPLE TO DRAMATICALLY INCREASE THE TIME WE ARE CONCIOUS, RATHER THAN OPERATING OUT OF OUR SUBCONCIOUS. ANYONE OF ANY BACKGROUND, INTELLIGENCE, OR EDUCATION CAN LEARN AND APPLY THIS RULE TO AID IN THEIR SUCCESS.

Turn to the next page to learn how...

<u>The Rule</u> - Invest 3% of every hour *(2 minutes)* at the end of every hour to briefly pause and reflect on what you just did for the last 58 minutes. Journal it on a single line, using notes only you will understand to stay under 2 minutes.

This will provide you will the following six benefits and competitive advantages over anyone who does not consistently utilize the Rule:

- Increased conscious time versus subconscious time
- Less anxiety
- Proactive effect – You will waste less time when *(and we all will)* hooked by entertainment, social media, or other distractions, because you know you need to log this activity at the end of the hour
- Longer and more frequent utilization of creative brainpower
- Significantly less "lost time"
- Seemingly superhuman levels of discipline and develop a reputation as a person who does what they said they would do when they said they would

The 3% Journal records the following:

- The date
- Commitments made
- Activities for all hour blocks

Throughout the day, any commitments you make to anyone go in the journal. Self-confidence is formed by how well we keep our promises to ourselves and others. When we meet confident people, that is a good thing. They are likely someone who keeps their promises.

At the end of the day, before sleep, review the day's notes, re-committing on outstanding commitments that you will follow through if not the next day, as soon as you can. While reviewing the actions taken within the hours, assess where inefficiencies or wasted time can be eliminated, and more useful, productive actions can instead be taken.

BEWARE: Once the Rule is learned, it must be applied to change your life. Knowledge of the Rule alone is not a silver bullet, but knowledge plus daily application will make you appear like a magician who can do things others can't.

BIG Why

Anyone who has watched Russel Crowe shout, *"ARE YOU NOT ENTERTAINED?"* in Gladiator, or any similar medieval times-era movie, knows that no soldier goes into battle with only a shield.

They also bring a sword. Our *Why* is that sword.

One truth about life: It is painful. We experience physical pain. We experience emotional pain. We experience spiritual pain. We experience betrayal.

And this is good.

Let me explain – without pain, happiness would cease to exist, and vice versa. Without losing, victory does not taste sweet. Without negative opposites, there is no intrinsic value in positives. Darkness is only the absence of light.

Life is about experiencing both good and bad emotions. One of my mentors, Ed, said that our lives are the quality of our emotions. How right he is!

The problem is that too many of us today bury bad emotions with TV, the bottom of a bottle, or a needle in the arm. Instead of accepting what we are feeling, and channeling that energy into creative action, we allow ourselves to "give up," and instead live a life dedicated to mindless entertainment and hedonistic pleasures.

The reason, I believe, that many of us choose to bury our emotions, rather than face them, is simply because we don't have a weapon to fight back with.

We must have a BIG *Why* when curveballs are thrown at our faces.

To decide what your Why is, you must remove every distraction from your environment. You must clear your mind best you can and focus on your heart. A why from the brain will surely die given enough time.

A why from the heart, though, will stand the test of time and adversity.

Now, I ask that you preferably get out in nature on a walk or a hike and let yourself ponder on why you do what you do for a living. Not the first, second, third, or fourth answer that crosses your mind, go deeper still.

To help – I will share my personal why below:

My why in life is to change the course of my family's legacy, and to help one million people change theirs. As a child I was never hungry, or anything dramatic, but I grew up in a family where it was always paycheck to paycheck. It wasn't until a long time ago that I learned the reasons that my family, and many others, suffer from this lifestyle.

I don't mean to sound ungrateful, and hope that it does not come off that way. I am well aware that many others have much less than I had as a kid. I do not mean any disrespect or mean to devalue anyone's experiences.

Remember, it is my hope to help empower others to provide more for their children and create a massive ripple effect that one day leads to your family becoming millionaires, and billionaires. True wealth is generational, and takes one person to stand up, and say, "I will take this responsibility and change things for the better. Someone has to."

Before I continue, let me be clear – There was never a lack of love in my family. I grew up well-supported and fulfilled in that regard. If it wasn't for my grandmother, I don't think this book would have ever been because she was the only one who read to me.

The primary reason my family has fallen into this lifestyle is because our belief in ourselves and our potential has been small. As far as I know, nobody before me has ever written down the goal of, *Own a private jet.* Because of this, nobody has owned a private jet.

So, you may think my why is to help people change their family financially-speaking, but you'd only be on the right track. What I want to do is help people change their Beliefs, Goals, Mentors, Associations, Habits, and Actions. When we change those six things, our lives change. On the next page I will share with you the cause of my addiction and what it did for my life.

Growing up in the situation I did, I was often outdoors; riding bicycles through the woods, playing sports, wrestling with friends, sword-fighting, and since I grew up in the Midwestern US, king of the hill in the wintertime along with snowball fights.

My addiction was created out of a gnawing hunger deep inside of me to explore, adventure, and see what was out there. I have always had a grand imagination, so when I would be outside in the forest, I would imagine myself in some far away land, exploring unknown lands.

What is inexpensive, and allows for countless hours of this exact sort of need to be satiated? Video games.

It is painful to admit the amount of time I lost to video games. But in the spirit of being a human that hopes this brutal honestly will help another human beat an addiction they might not even yet realize they have; I will expose myself bare now.

In my assessment, I lost a full four to five years of actual real life during my addiction. Yes, that is right. I mean for that amount of time I was sitting in front of a computer or console.

Yes, I did yield many benefits and learning experiences, believe it or not. I learned that people working together toward a shared goal or future have a lot power. I learned that hard work works. I learned that I am a leader. I learned that I receive a ton of fulfillment and happiness from helping others grow, learn, and expand their potential. I learned that a life well-invested for me means I have helped others invest their lives well.

World of Warcraft, thank you for the experience as a raid leader, "commanding the troops," helping 24 other people on a 25-person team reach elite raider status. Even though it was digital, the level of commitment that this game takes to reach that level and defeat the hardest bosses that the game has to offer is extraordinary. It takes people dedicated to maximizing what they can do, and it takes an unbelievable amount of time and practice. This commitment does not come freely from the people in your guild, it must be earned by strong leadership that truly cares about their people getting to the places where they want to go. I took that responsibility seriously and mastered my role as a raid leader.

At a point in my life, I realized much of what made me successful at this game would make me successful in real life, once I started applying them outside of the video game, and in the real world.

To circle back and close this chapter – I do not wish this addiction on my children as a result of me failing to realize a better future for them. I will bring forth a reality where instead of dreaming of going places, we will actually go places together, sharing and creating real memories in the real world. To do this, I must possess more financial resources than my father had, and to achieve that, I need to help many more people than he did.

I believe that this formula I have shared with you will equip you with the most powerful tool that you can have in your wheelhouse to help you author the life you want to create. That tool is Awareness of how Conscious we are at any given moment of the day.

Beware: Without a Big Why it is impossible to avoid being pulled off course when we are faced with a major unexpected challenge in our lives. Similarly, without a Big Why we drift aimlessly through life. Sure, we can continue to advance through our careers, have children, and hit all the checkboxes, but unless we have a burning reason in our hearts in why we're doing these things, we are always at risk of living a life unfulfilled.

Prepare well by committing yourself fully to a powerful enough Why that will carry you through the darkness that is surely coming. *(But don't forget, the light is also surely coming – get through the darkness – keep swinging your sword until you see light breakthrough)*

BIG Goals

With a clear and Big Why, the next thing we must track is how well we are progressing toward realizing our Goals. What are your goals? If you do not have these written down somewhere you can look at them when you need them, it would benefit you greatly to invest the time into writing out this list. It doesn't have to be a massive one; just come up with five 1-year, five 5-year, and five 10-year goals.

Again, this isn't just metaphorical or a "good idea." Go forth, create your list, and have fun doing it!

Consider this – You are at work, and you lose a deal. You go to your car, and you see you have a flat tire. You are walking down the sidewalk, looking at your phone, and you walk into a pole.

These situations are all rightfully frustrating for their own reasons, except you, phone person, you deserved to walk into that pole. Pay attention!

It is easy in these situations to allow our moods to sour, for much longer than they should. How do we combat this from happening to us?

Any time we find ourselves slipping into negative thoughts, we must remember *why* we are doing what we are doing.

Then, we must put our minds back into positive thoughts, and to do that, our minds need us to plant a positive seed.

Our goals list contains positive seeds for us to choose from, any time of the day, at no additional cost to us. No monthly subscription, or upgrades required. Just a pen, and a piece of paper.

The goals list is the armor we wear, that when paired with a powerful *Why*, protects us from spiralizing into time-wasting negativity. It also provides us with a much-needed boost when life throws us its inevitable challenges. On a rainy day, we can pull out our goals list, and remember why we get out bed every day.

As my friend, Ian from Missouri, put it, *"It's hard to get out of a situation as long as you continue to look through shit-covered goggles."* Too true, old friend. I can't tell you how many times I've remembered that saying and it got me out of a negative thought cycle. I'm grateful you said those words so many years ago.

Here is the deal about goals though – they don't happen for nothing. Nothing is free.

When we are setting our goals, we have to also set our sacrifices or what we will trade to reach those goals. Expecting something for nothing violates one of the laws of this life. We must be clear and transparent about what cost we will pay for what we want.

Last thing about goals – set by when dates.

We have to give our best guess to when we want to have something by, otherwise our subconscious mind has too much leeway. It is no different if a boss gives a worker a task, but no deadline. If the worker has a pile of other tasks, there is no telling when that new task will get done.

Is that any way to approach the goals we really want? Let's be clear when we want something by, so our minds can work in the background to create it for us.

BEWARE: Without Big Goals we are vulnerable to despair, time-wasting thought, and allowing ourselves to settle into mediocrity. Do not forget – there is no such thing as something for nothing. All prices must be paid in full.

Mentors

Who we choose to ask for advice is probably the most overlooked aspect of success we mess up. I believe that George S. Clason said it perfectly in The Richest Man in Babylon - *"Don't trust a bricklayer to buy jewels."*

Unfortunately, many of us do just that. We seek counsel from people with opinions, rather than experts with concrete steps to success that we can follow.

This, I believe, is what squashes grand ideas. Someone with a big, powerful imagination dreams up something radical, and shares it with their happy hour friends. A few beers later, and the idea has died before it ever had a chance to change lives.

We want to take great care in who we choose to ask for help. Successful people are generally humbled and grateful for an opportunity to share their experience and wisdom with the young, hungry up-and-coming student of success.

Seek out someone who is ten years older, twenty years older, and thirty years older. Seek yet another who is in another field or industry, and one more that is in your own field or industry. Having mentors will move us forward through life leaps and bounds.

Nothing comes free – you too must provide something valuable to their life they did not have before they met you.

Be creative and be persistent.

Another foul we commit when it comes to mentors, is that many of us don't ever seek them out. Just like the book we don't read can't help us, thank you Jim Rohn for your legendary level of wisdom, the mentor we aren't connected to cannot teach us.

I can testify that it is worth 3x-10x or beyond whatever financial cost you must pay to be a part of a life accelerator program with proven leaders in whatever it is they are trying to help people with. For example, under the mentorship of Andy Frisella and Ed Mylett, my capacity has exponentially grown. The kind of mentorship I am referring to is listening to Andy's MFCEO and Real AF podcast and Ed's The Ed Mylett Show podcast – and also by investing in the Arete accelerator.

These men are 100% committed to making this world a better place then they found it. They already have, and they're going to do so much more. I believe in their mission – they will improve the world by improving the business world. They are leaving a legacy that will be remembered.

BEWARE: Going it alone through life will only slow our progress to the best version of ourselves. Having coaches in our corner with a vested interest in our success will produce such results in our life that people without coaches will be left scratching their heads at how we are moving forward with such momentum.

Associations

Two sides to the same coin as mentors, our associations are foundational to the person we become. These are the people we interact with most often and influence us the most.

We must guard well our associations. These people are the individuals we are forging our lives with. If we share our time with people who are complainers, can't-do'ers, or would've-done'ers, then we too shall become this caliber of person.

On the other hand, if we share our time with people that know that limitations in this life are truly self-inflicted, that we are the ones who hold ourselves back, then we are in good company. These people are surely big dreamers, have big plans, and follow them up with big actions. These people are also consistent in their day to day habits, and this is important.

Our associations will either hold us accountable to the things we say are important, or want in our lives, or they will not. Imagine – spending *(wasting)* our time with people that laugh at us, or tell us to *"be more realistic,"* if we tell them we will one day be an executive in our organization. The best thing we can do with these people is delete their contact information from our phone and stop wasting our time with them.

We owe it to ourselves to instead surround ourselves with people that would answer with, *"OK, I like that idea. How will you achieve this? When will you be an executive? What ideas do you have to start making major improvements to the business, so that current executive leadership will learn your name through your performance alone?"*

Now, imagine that life. Which one would you rather have? But do you really...? You know what you need to do, if you mean it. I know, it will be hard. It IS hard. But if you're serious about creating a better future for yourself, your family, your real friends, and your legacy, there is no more important sacrifice to be made.

BEWARE: An inability or reluctance to shed bad relationships will impair our step, as the ship is impaired by an anchor. We must unshackle our anchor as soon as we are aware it is an anchor. It may be difficult at first, but it will be the best thing we can do for our future. Stay strong and earn friendships with people that really care.

Habits

After we have selected well the people we will create a better world with, now we must choose what habits will serve us. Remember well, our habits either serve us or they betray us. Which one it is depends entirely on us.

Here are six fantastic books on habits that will surely lead to a successful life if implemented – *Success Habits* by Napoleon Hill, *Million Dollar Habits* by Brian Tracy, *The 7 Habits of Highly Effective People* by Stephen Covey, *The Power of Habit* by Charles Duhigg, *Atomic Habits* by James Clear, and *High Performance Habits* by Brendon Burchard.

Our habits are like the engine of our life's ship. Bad habits will cause us to trudge along through life as if we're driving through mud in a storm, while good habits will power us along through life as if we're wearing a jetpack and flying over all the chaos.

The reason the rule is so powerful is because of how powerful habits are. When we are not operating out of our conscious minds, we are in autopilot going through the motions operating out of our subconscious minds.

Even with the rule, we will still be operating out of this subconscious often, so it is crucial we have strong habits set in stone that we default to when we go into our subconscious operating patterns. We have to set ourselves up for success in advance.

Here are a handful of habits that are sure to help us in our lives if we do them every day:

Read ten pages of a personal improvement book & share what you learn with at least one other person, drink a gallon of water, workout for 45 minutes, follow a diet *(one cheat meal per week),* eat a vegetable, eat a fruit, and track your finances every morning & evening. Thank you, Andy, for 75 hard.

The same reason why many of us don't know where our money goes is the same as why we lose time. We don't budget it or track it.

BEWARE: Our habits are our most powerful allies or our worst enemies when it comes to our success. Once they are set, they are challenging to change. We must be intentional with choosing what habits we will live by, for they will make or break us.

Actions, Are Yours Positive or Negative?

Everything we have discussed up to this point in the book is for naught, unless it is followed up by actions. A dream without action is just a dream.

We should live like we are sharks; if we stop swimming, we will die. Every night when we go to bed, we recharge our "gas tanks" and start the next day fresh. Yet, many of us go through our days as if we have the governor set at 20 miles per hour, or 32.19 kilometers per hour, when we should be humming in the power band.

Why choose anything but maximum effort, if you're a Deadpool fan, Max Out if you listen to Ed Mylett, or 100 to 0 if you listen to Andy Frisella?

Maximum effort will yield us two things – the best possible versions of ourselves, and the best possible lives for ourselves. With the real possibility that we only get one life, unlike cats, lucky bastards, why not choose the greatest one we can have?

Choose greatness.

Life is meant to be lived, and that means taking one step after the other. I know, this all sounds pretty basic stuff, yet it is worth repeating, because I'm taking this another direction.

If you're in sales and you get a phone call that you lost a major deal, what do you do? Do you groan and moan the rest of the day, or do you grab your prospect list and begin looking for another grand opportunity, using what you learned on this failure, so you can earn the next one?

If you're an athlete and you permanently injure yourself, will your identity completely fall to pieces, or will your why power you through, leading you instead to a life of coaching, where your experience & ability can be transferred and duplicated to others?

When I'm talking about actions, what I'm really talking about is, what do we do when things do not go our way? We don't always get to choose what happens to us, but we do always choose how we respond to this adversity. There are two choices – Positive or Negative. Do not let anyone fool you; there are no neutral choices in life. Either your constructive, or you're deconstructive.

You're part of the problem, or you're part of the solution. Which side of the equation we're on depends entirely on what we do immediately after receiving bad news.

Bad news can infect us like a cancer. If we allow something out of our control to control what we do moving forward, we are plagued. This sickness grows in difficulty to purge the longer it stays inside of us.

BEWARE: We will perform actions whether we are conscious of them, or whether we are not. That is the power of habits at play, and why everything else we have discussed up to this point has been shared in the progression that it has been. Each chapter builds on the next, because without the rest, our actions will be random. We will live without intentionality. We must choose to be intentional in everything we do.

Stop Trying to Change Emotions, Start Changing the Meaning to Events

Too many of us try to change our emotions. This is impossible, and what leads to much wasted time.

We cannot change how we feel, but we can change the meaning we have associated to events in our lives.

Remember this: Events -> Meanings

We choose what meaning an event has for us. Does this work even in extreme scenarios? Absolutely! What about that car accident that left us paralyzed from the waist down (for those of you this has happened to, my heart aches for what you have to deal with on a daily basis) ? Will we fall to despair that we may never walk again with our own legs, or do we focus on the new opportunity we have to be a living example for others in our shoes that despite all circumstances, we choose to live well.

I know – it is undoubtedly easier said than done for many of us living with chronic ailments. Regardless, as hard as it may be to accept it right now, where you are at and facing, it is the truth. We cannot always choose what happens to us, only if we react positively or negatively.

BEWARE: Positive mindset is more than listening to motivational audios every day (even though that is a great idea); it is being aware and remembering that we are the masters of our fate. We choose if we are positive or if we are negative. Whether our lives are positive or negative simply comes down to how often we respond with one or the other as events happen to us.

Culture

"Culture eats strategy for breakfast." – Peter Drucker

How true is that? There are countless examples of organizations that know this, and ensure they focus daily on the health of their culture. These are the Fortune 50, 100 and 500 companies.

These organizations have all three elements necessary: The are Energized, Engaged, and Enabled. (The "Three E's", from All In by Gostick and Elton)

Simply put: Engaged people feel an attachment to the company and willingness to give extra effort. Enabled people have a work environment that supports productivity and performance. Energized people believe that their leaders provide individual, physical, social, and emotional well-being at work.

Companies with all three have the highest loyalty in both their employees and customers. They have the highest revenues and profit margins. They deliver high-performance and big results year over year.

We all have experienced great culture at some point in our lives, even if we're in the unfortunate group that has never personally experienced it at a company we've worked at (the majority).

Examples, in no particular order: Nordstrom, Apple, Southwest Airlines, 1stPhorm, and Zappos.

These organizations are all 100% people (customer)-focused first and foremost. Everything else stems from that truth.

What has this resulted in? Incredibly high customer loyalty. This is the surest path to continued success over the long game, and they play it best.

Similar to leadership, culture can be (and is) influenced from any (every) position within the organization. Like bad news, or bad experiences, bad culture spreads faster than good culture.

This is why it is crucial that the leadership of an organization expedites surgical removal of any cancerous individuals.

Cancer is defined by one or both of these traits: Toxicity or Complacency.

One alone will tank a person's ability to positively impact a business, while both will turn someone into a person who rapidly erodes the efforts and progress of the business.

If you have leadership in your organization that turns an eye on toxic or complacent people, you should run fast. On a long enough timeline, I will be genuinely surprised if they survive over the next couple decades without serious and drastic change, and fast.

Lack of action on leadership's behalf in this scenario is a combination of:

Ineffective + No integrity + No vision + No core values + No care about their people

In my life, though I've only been a part of two organizations in my sales career, before that I went through many short-term jobs from 16-21. During that time and in my time in sales, I have been a part of many different cultures.

Do not settle for a poor culture, or a company with poor leadership – it will drain your soul and limit your progress to success and the life you want.

Be a positive factor in the organization's culture that you're a part of. It makes life better, work more fun, and will certainly get the attention of great leaders. That will eventually lead to more opportunities for advancement and career growth.

Napoleon Hill said it better than I ever could.

"The man who does more than he is paid for will soon be paid for more than he does."

Now that is powerful!

BEWARE: Avoiding culture will at best cripple business and personal growth. At worst, it will decimate business and personal growth, causing a backward spiral. Focus on learning, studying, and applying best practices for healthy culture, and it will pay back the highest **ROI** that any investment can in an organization.

Leadership

Leadership is what everything rises and falls on. Whether we are talking about our own personal lives, or an organization, a large portion of our attention should be aimed at how well they are ran by their leaders.

In the case of our own lives – we must first lead ourselves well, before we can ever expect to lead others well. This means everything we do is important. But only if we believe that to be true.

How many of us would raise our hands if asked – "The last time you went to the gym, how many of you saw scraps of paper all over the bathroom/locker room floors?"

I would guess that the % would be over half.

So here is my question: If we can't trust someone to be a decent human and pick up their paper when they miss the garbage, or if we have the suspicion they think themselves too high to help pick up others' garbage scraps on the locker room floors, will we consider them an effective leader that we want to follow and build with?

Likely not.

Yet, why do so many people walk by these countless opportunities to help clean one of the environments that serves them, in helping them achieve their lifestyle and fitness goals? The opportunity to help make this important environment a more fulfilling environment, by taking some ownership over it.

Try it – Next time you see scraps on the floor, when you're done washing your hands, use your paper to pick up one or a few pieces on the floor before you toss yours in the trash. Do these enough times, and you will bear witness to a chain effect of suddenly seeing other members of the gym doing the same.

Another analogy to help here – Not many people want to be the first person to clap to applaud a fantastic performance; the majority prefers to wait for when it is safe to clap and not get embarrassed.

This holds true for leadership – The people who pick up others' trash, and the people who aren't afraid to risk clapping prematurely are often people who have leadership DNA within them.

Investing in developing as a leader is critical to one's current and future success. There are countless books out there on leadership, but if I had to make one recommendation that someone could binge on, rather than that self-defeating "affordable" monthly TV subscription, it would be John C. Maxwell. This man is a legend in leadership, and has provided millions with his experience, wisdom, and lessons. You would be well-rewarded by taking the time to learn well what Mr. Maxwell has to teach on this topic.

But as with all things, learning alone does nothing. We must apply and try what we are learning in the real world, with real people. We must make real mistakes to learn from, and on the flip side, see and feel the genuine emotion from someone who is being well-led.

We need to begin to lead from whatever station we are at, wherever we work. Why? All good things of the world come from somewhere in the entrepreneurial space. For the world to improve, the entrepreneurial space must be pure.

Consider this – If all business owners, leaders in business, and managers within those businesses considered (and realized it was) it their duty to help all the people they work with not only succeed professionally, but also personally, then eventually a momentum would be created that would generate a massive positive change in the world.

The business feeds the families, the families feed their family and their friends, then those people who have been fed continue to feed those in their social circles of influence, and so on. You can see the ripples spreading.

When seeking employment or an organization to plant a stake at, it is important to take time to research the leadership team. An organization rarely exceeds the level of the leadership. On the other hand, it is just downright a pain in the ass going into work every day where there is weak or no real leadership. There are a lot of managers today in leadership positions, and it is going to ruin a lot of businesses. And I don't mean just P&L statements, I mean literally end businesses.

Leadership and Culture go together just like trees and good soil do. Leaders are the soil, and trees are the culture that grow from the organization's leadership. What we plant must grow – if the leadership is not focused or does not prioritize culture, the organization is ultimately doomed unless the employees or front-line level managers rally on their own and form a culture themselves.

This is why great leaders are so well-rewarded in terms of material things. But more importantly, they are more well-rewarded in terms of fulfillment, happiness, and friendships.

Leaders are foundational to the success of an organization, everyone in it, every vendor-partner that does business with them, and the list continues for quite some time. Leaders create the world the rest just live in as spectators.

Remember: Leadership does not mean titles or positions. Leadership is how well you influence others to believe in their potential and help them believe they can become the best version of themselves. Do not think for a second, I don't think any position on the planet cannot exemplify great leadership and show others by example what it means to lead well. Anybody can be a leader, regardless of age or title.

Beware: Ignorance is no absolution of guilt. Not developing one's leadership ability is not only wasting one's own potential, but also wasting a lifetime worth of opportunities to help other people avoid wasting theirs.

A Portion of Everything You Earn is Yours to Keep

Also, from The Richest Man in Babylon is the most simple and sound financial advice I've ever heard. I feel I would be remiss if I didn't share this wisdom, for those readers that have not yet read that book. 'A portion of everything we earn is ours to keep.'

If we work and earn income, and never save any of it, we will forever remain at risk to life's unforeseen events. We are vulnerable, because if we become unable to earn money, our money runs out. We could end up homeless, divorced, or lose our kids.

The surest path to avoiding this pitfall is to save at least 10% of everything we earn. If we can't start there, start with even 1%, if it has to be. Gradually increase over time. Set it up so that this % automatically is removed from each check before you see the money and pretend it doesn't exist. But don't just save for saving's sake.

Instead, stockpile. Stockpile toward a planned investment that will be a cash-flow or income-producing asset. At a point we will have enough of these assets that we and our family are well-protected from unforeseen circumstances.

BEWARE: Not having the philosophy that a portion of everything we earn is ours to keep will doom us to living paycheck to paycheck, with less than $5,000 in an emergency fund, for the rest of our lives. We have to change our philosophy before we can change our actions and standard of living.

Budgeting

Here is a simple formula to get away from working for money, and have your money begin working for you (money likes to make babies with other money – that is the purpose for which it was invented).

Here is the plan *(adaptation of Jim Rohn's teachings; I added a 6-month savings)*

Save (stockpile) 10% of everything we earn until we have 6 months' worth of living expenses, all-in. If every source of income went away suddenly, we need to be able to live for 6 months with zero stress, while we figure out our next move. This keeps us in an abundance state of mind, and we will find another place to build a life much easier and faster. Desperation is the recipe for failure.

Invest 10% into Active investments (real estate; tangible assets that generate cash flow; capital gains). For most of us, we must save 10% of everything we earn and build a bucket of money over time. We can't go to the bank with $100 in hand and ask for a loan for $300,000 to get a duplex lot. But we can probably get that loan with $60,000 down and good credit.

Invest 10% into Passive investments (loan your money to others to make that money grow for you with little thought or involvement on your part). Our active investments will take focus and time, while this bucket is still highly profitable long-term, and requires barely any thought or time. It keeps us diversified, and also has the added benefit of building partnerships with people as our investment amount grows to considerable size. Once that happens, they will eventually take note, because we are helping them grow their business to such a big degree.

Give 10% to Charity. This one is simple – if we don't give $10 for every $100, we earn; we will never give $100,000 when we earn our first million. I can't explain it, but once I adopted the "two-dollar" concept with tipping, or giving, my life changed. I started making more money, and random discounts and even "free" money came out of nowhere at unexpected times. If we're going to tip someone a dollar, give them two. If we're thinking about giving them a 15% tip, make it 20%. (I always tip 20% minimum)

We will feel better doing this. The person receiving the tip will feel better. This inexpensive extra amount will generate so much positive energy that keeps expanding well beyond the extra few bucks, that eventually that energy returns to us in amplified fashion. Give $3 today to a homeless person, and someday an opportunity will come in where we can earn $300. Give someone $100 today, and we will suddenly find 10 great opportunities to earn $100 each and build lifetime relationships with each that will lead to more money for the rest of your life.

Don't live on more than 60-70% of your income. Once the 6 months survival egg is built, we can shift that money back into standard of living, or invest into one of our two buckets, or both buckets. That is our choice – by having 6 months of living expenses saved, we are way ahead of the pack. Most people are a car accident or hospital bill away from being on the streets.

Budget every paycheck or earnings and have a monthly budget. Yes – do both. Let me explain – we should absolutely have a plan for our money in advance of getting static, regular income. But we should also make another specific budget every time the money actually comes into our bank accounts before a dollar is used.

If we fail to plan in advance where our dollars will go, our dollars will go where they want to go. We will be one of those people who say, "I don't know where it all goes." "It just seems to get away from me." "I can never seem to get ahead."

Taking the time to plan where every dollar will go is what wealthy people do. Making buckets is a good idea – plan to spend a specific amount every month on a category. Eating out, groceries, entertainment, education, unexpected breakdown/repair bucket, and advertising are just a handful of examples. Once the money for a particular category is cashed out, you have to have the willpower and not do that thing until you make more money.

What if we go over or mess up? That's okay! Everyone that is reading this is human. (If you're actually an alien, please, share this with your home planet so even more can benefit from what I'm sharing.)

If we make a mistake and go over, just move some of that money from a different category into that "oops" category. Now we're still being focused on where our money is going. Like time, money requires awareness, or both pull a Houdini on us.

BEWARE: We must remain vigilant of our dollars. Refusing to participate in budgeting will likely leave us stuck in a cycle of paycheck to paycheck. This is an exceptionally vulnerable position to be in and is entirely avoidable with discipline.

Authenticity

Another key ingredient to success in business and dating is being your authentic self. When you try to copy someone else you will carry yourself awkwardly. Just be you.

With social media, I doubt there has ever been a time where copycats have ever been more rampant. We see people who appear to be living the dream life, or the life we would want to be experiencing anyways, and we think if we act like them, talk like them, and walk like them, we will live like them. Far from it. You will just come off as a phony.

On the other side of that, when you embrace who you are you will radiate a proper charisma. There is only one unique you, let that person shine to the world.

Yes, being authentic will cost you opportunities, but it will gain you many more than you will lose. You can't make everyone like you. But those that do like you will really like you.

Take Chick-Fil-A for example – whether you love them or hate them, you can't argue that they do not have an ultra-successful business model. With 10.5 billion in sales in 2019 with just about 2,500 locations, compared to McDonalds at 38.5 billion in sales with roughly 14,000 locations, you can see how much more they accomplish with less.

That means that Chick-Fil-A produces an average of $4,200,000 worth of sales per location while McDonalds produces an average of $2,750,000 worth of sales per location. Math and results do not lie.

How does Chick-Fil-A accomplish this? They completely embrace who they are as an organization. They make their values and what they stand for loud and clear. They don't placate every possible customer. This allows people to choose to rally behind their cause or disagree and choose to eat somewhere else.

Those that do rally are fiercely loyal. Loyalty is the number one goal as a salesperson.

On the dating side, and this is a big reason the bar scene is a poor choice for finding someone who will mesh well with you, authenticity is important.

One of the biggest reasons the divorce rate is so high in the US is due to a lack of authenticity. People try to be who they think the other person will like. Then when that dopamine rush of the honeymoon stage wears off, and the mask comes off, people have a confused look on their face as if they're seeing the other person for the first time.

In a way, they are.

You stand to save a lot of time by being authentic with potential dating partners. Not only yours, but theirs as well. Being authentic is a way of being respectful.

Intent

What we have in our hearts and souls shows on the outside. If all you want is a quick sale, it will show. If you don't care what the outcome of you selling something to a client is, it will show. If you don't have belief in yourself, company, or solution, it will show.

If you have the best interests of the customer in mind, they will feel that. If you are genuinely interested in producing the highest value outcome for your customer, it will be palpable. If you want to help them win and succeed, they will feel good around you.

Our inner thoughts drive what we do in our actions.

Tomorrow is Not Promised

We get one opportunity in life. No second chances or extra lives. One shot.

Refuse to die an unlived life.

Les Brown said something once that really stuck with me for a long while. "If you died this very moment, what will die with you? What dreams? What ideas? What talents? What leadership potential? What greatness that you showed up to bring? That you allowed fear or procrastination to hold you back. Only to realize that you never lived, only to realize that you've never scraped the surface of your potential."

Now that is a sobering thought. It is also a fantastic question. We would all greatly benefit if we took this question to heart and answered it.

Sometimes we are all guilty of getting too caught up in the past or the future. The catch is that the future and past do not exist. They are only real in our minds.

By spending too much of our energy in the past or the future, we are unable to invest our energy into the eternal present now. And now is all that we have.

We are all limited in how much energy we can expend on a daily basis. That is why it is important to remain as present as possible throughout each day. How present we are will decide what our future lives will be.

If we are not present, we will be stuck in autopilot, coasting through the days with our engrained habits, good or bad. That isn't much different than leaving our fate to chance.

Rather than leave it to chance, we can be the captain of our fate. Doesn't that sound better?

Our lives can be considered as if we are a ship, and the engine is always running. We are always going in one direction or another, regardless if we are actively steering the ship or not, the ship will continue moving.

We can choose to remain on the deck, hands on the wheel, or we can allow ourselves to go under the deck, and in the dark.

If we choose to go under the deck, our lives will be similar to a ship that leaves the harbor with no destination, it will either sink or end up on a deserted island.

Choose to remain on the deck, though, and we have great power over the course of our lives.

Never forget, you are the captain of your ship. Go into each day with eyes wide open, hands on the wheel, and headed in the direction of your choosing.

Drifting

As human beings, we are all at risk of drifting. I'm borrowing the definition of this word from Napoleon Hill, because it is too good to not share here in the case you have never heard of Napoleon Hill, or read his book, Outwitting the Devil.

There are a handful of ways to know if we are drifting. If you can answer in the affirmative to any of these, then it is probable that you are drifting, and should snap out of it now.

If we are being pushed mostly by fear, we are drifting. If we must be forced or ordered by someone else to do something, and lack enthusiasm or drive, we are drifting. If we continue to make the same mistakes over and over again, we are drifting. If we begin many things without finishing them, we are drifting. If we are overeating and not exercising, we are drifting. If we criticize others, either in our own mind or publicly, we are drifting. And the biggest one of all, if we lack a major purpose in life, we are drifting.

Drifting is extremely dangerous to us because it leads us down roads that are difficult to get off of. Addiction, homelessness, jail, or stuck in a loveless relationship are a few examples of where we can find ourselves if we drift too long.

This is why having friends around us that will tell us what we need to hear rather than what we want to hear is so important.

Comfort and complacency will also lead to drifting eventually. That is why so many marriages (at least in the

US) lead to one or both people becoming overweight, or obese.

It is also why the two people that get into the most car accidents are those that are new to it, or those that have been driving for a long time. The former is comfortable in a way because they have never been in an accident, and do not know how bad it hurts or how much it can set you back. The latter is comfortable because they have gone for so long without any incidents, that they begin to grow complacent.

The fastest way to get ourselves out of a drift is to tell friends that we are in a rut. They will be able to see our blind spots and inspire us to snap out of it. Another fast way out is to take massive action. And I mean the kind of action that is radical. It will force your brain to adapt to the sudden change, and it will be like a Corvette that is all warmed up.

I would be remiss if I didn't suggest that if you have not already read Outwitting the Devil, your time would be well-invested if you pick it up and read it. There is so much wisdom in all of Hill's work, but this one is my favorite. He is my favorite author.

If my book found you while you are in a state of drifting, it is my sincerest hope that these words get you out of the drift. There is nothing more perilous to us than drifting.

Enrolling Others

One of the best skills any of us can learn and develop is enrolling others. To enroll someone means to move, touch, and inspire them.

The first thing to know about enrollment is that it is best done by our voice. It can be done through writing as well, but writing does not carry the same energy that voice does. Text messaging or email are both poor choices when it comes to enrollment.

We have all watched or listened to someone that has left the hairs on our arms or backs standing up. Someone that really captivated us to the point that we acted after they were done. They enrolled us with their message.

The reason that voice is the best method of enrolling others is because it is the most human form of communication. It connects us those that are listening to us.

In our modern world voice communication has become all the more valuable. With how many people text their friends and families "Happy Birthdays" instead of picking up the phone to call them, when someone does call it really catches our attention.

That is one of those things that is unfortunate about the technological advances of our day. People have become ultra-lazy in communication. Most are completely unaware of what kind of message it sends to someone when they text them about something on an important day.

Our ability to enroll others will drive a lot of our life experiences. Some may read this chapter and think this is essentially our ability to sell others. And while there is an element of selling, it cheapens what enrollment is to call it selling. It goes well beyond what selling is.

When someone does a good job at selling someone, occasionally they leave the person in a state of being moved, touched, and inspired.

But when someone enrolls another, by definition the other person has most certainly been left moved, touched, and inspired.

And that is one the things we are here to do – inspire others to become more than they are today. One of the best feelings in the world is when someone tells us that we helped them in a big way.

I recall a time when one of my old friends from middle school that I had not spoken to since we had graduated high school sent me a message on social media. In that message he recounted a time when he had been walking home, and he got bullied.

He asked me if I would walk with him after school and I said I would. That day we were walking, the bullies returned, and I stood them down.

Here is the thing about this, when he messaged me, I was surprised, because I had forgotten I had even done this for him. That is one of the beautiful aspects of life – we never know what our actions will mean to someone. This had happened a long time ago, but it had meant so much to him that he never forgot it.

After this, he joined the school wrestling team and became one of the best wrestlers in our state. He decided he would not be bullied any longer, and instead chose to become the kind of person that could and would stand up to bullies for others.

My empathy and decision to act enrolled him in another reality for himself.

The true power of enrollment is that it allows us to change other people's lives.

Connection

To piggyback the previous chapter, too many of us spend too much time alone. In a weird way, our brains think that we're getting connection from social media and texting, but our souls do not.

I believe one of the main drivers for the increased rate of people prescribed to anti-anxiety or anti-depression medications is due in large part to how disconnected we are from each other.

As human beings we are social creatures. We crave the attention, touch, and laughter of another human being. We want to be heard by other human beings. That is one area where texting lacks severely. We cannot truly hear or see the other person's reaction to our joke or our message.

One of the best sounds we get to experience is someone's laughter. That is completely left out in all forms of communication other than voice. When we see someone's eyes light up when they're around us, that too is missed without being face to face.

Who is someone you haven't seen or spoken with in a while? Why not pick up the phone and give them a call? Today is a fine day to reconnect with them.

You will be glad you did.

Comfort Will Kill You

In this society we have the kinds of luxuries that only the kings of the past had. Luxuries that we take for granted. Refrigerators, air conditioning, heating, running clean water to drink and shower with, grocery stores, cell phones, microwaves, dishwashers, washers and dryers.

All of these make our lives significantly better than they would be without them. They are efficient, safe, and in the case of cell phones, gives us a dopamine hit whenever we want one.

All these also kill us. The reason why is because they make us comfortable.

"The worst thing that can happen to a person is to become civilized." - David Goggins.

There is truth to that statement.

Look at the current obesity, heart disease, and diabetes rates in the United States. Obesity is at 35% in nine states, 30% in 31 states, and 25% in 48 states. Heart disease remains the number one cause of death, accounting for one out of every three deaths. Nearly 800,000 Americans have a new or repeat stroke every year, with 90% of the risk due to modifiable risk factors, and 74% due to behavior. Over thirty million Americans have diabetes, and a quarter of them don't even know they have it. Over one-third of the population has prediabetes, and 90% of them don't know they have it.

As the saying goes, not all that glitters glows.

These comforts have helped the United States to these staggering statistics. Our obsession with removing pain, difficulty, and struggle is killing us.

Even marriage has its downfalls in this regard. With the comfort of the partnership, many couples become overweight over time. Without needing to look their best anymore (so they think) they begin to let some of their behaviors slide. And because they love one another, it is rare that a partner will tell the other person that they are getting fat. When in reality, if they did, it would mean they really love them.

There are many ways to combat this wave that is building year over year.

We can choose to use the stairs instead of the elevator or escalator. We can park further away from the store. Instead of the fried option we can go with the grilled option. We can eat vegetables in the morning and in the evening. We can eat fruit every morning. We can exercise every day for at least 45 minutes. A five-minute cold shower every morning has significant benefits for reducing the inflammation we have inflicted on ourselves from our bad decisions. It also replaces the need for caffeine for some people. Not that caffeine is bad, but it is yet another thing that most Americans overdo.

Mostly, though, we can be honest with ourselves and with others. We sugarcoat the truth too often nowadays. We are so caught up with avoiding conflict that we don't tell people what they really need to hear.

A person from east Asia told me, "Only in the United States do people lie to themselves about how fat the country is getting. Americans are nice to each other about how fat they are. It is so different from where I'm from." It is curious to think that we went from our forefathers who risked everything, the exact opposite of comfort, to arrive where we are today where we promote body positivity to the point that it is toxic. This positivity is leading to negative results for many people.

Where is this comfort leading us? If you have seen the movie Wall-E, you have your answer. That movie was chilling to me, because it could actually happen.

There is so much to be gained from choosing to be uncomfortable. Overcoming discomfort produces healthy dopamine, unlike alcohol or drugs. Overcoming discomfort leads to real self-confidence. Overcoming discomfort leads to us being capable.

Grit is the number one predictor of success. If you are swimming in comfort, it is likely you either don't have grit, or are on the path to losing it.

If you are currently stuck in living comfortably, choose to do something uncomfortable today. You will thank yourself immediately after you conquer the discomfort, and also in the future if you stay the course.

Your life literally depends on it.

Gratitude

If we are not grateful for what we have now, we will almost surely never have the things we wish we had in the future. Why would the universe grant us what we desire when we spit in the face of what we do have?

If there is no other takeaway from this book outside of the rule, it would be my wish for you to adopt a grateful morning and a grateful evening mindset. When you wake up, think of three things you're grateful for, and when you go to bed, think of three things you're grateful for. You will be shocked at the difference this habit makes in your life.

Your Word

Our word is all we have in this life. When we say something, people expect us to see it through to completion. When we fall short or fail this, their trust for us is damaged.

So, when we make a promise or commitment, we must deliver, and deliver well.

Think about it. What do we all share in common? We can all create our realities with our words and the commitments we make. We forge our futures in our language.

More on that in the next chapter.

What do we do when we make a promise and fail to deliver? We clean it up promptly, and either admit we should have never made the promise, or we make a new promise and don't let the person we committed to down again.

We're all human, we're all going to fail on a promise at some point. The important part is what we do after we fail. Do we just let it slide, or do we own it and fix it?

We fix it. We go beyond just doing what we originally said we would do, we exceed expectations. Because when we do that, we probably establish even more trust than we would have if we would have just fulfilled the original commitment.

Doing the Work

Have you ever wanted to just quit whatever it was you were doing and go to bed? Have you ever started a run and thought to yourself that you just wanted to stop running and walk instead?

Of course, you have.

Our brains are here for one reason – survival.

They will trick us into thinking we are tired when we're not. They will try to confuse us when we are doing something that is uncomfortable.

What would Jocko Willink say in a moment like this? "Good."

When we choose to overcome our brains and do the work, that is when we find massive growth. We become something more than we were before.

Doing the work creates dopamine in our brains when we finish the task, whereas if we decide to throw in the towel prematurely, we feel disappointed in ourselves.

What have you been putting off that you could decide to do the work today?

Go and do the work. Get it done. Do what you said you would do.

There is no reason to wait, no advantage or gain to be had by waiting.

Doing the work consistently over time compounds. It creates a positive snowball effect where we can build great momentum toward our goals.

The Example That Dogs Give Us

Dogs are the best example on the planet of what true gratitude and living fully present looks like. No matter what activity they are doing, they are fully engaged and love every moment of it. Especially Golden Retrievers, with their giant dog smiles.

We would all benefit to take a page from our four-legged friends. The more present we are, the more fulfilled and happier we are. It is when we get lost in the past or caught up in the future that stress enters our lives.

The more we focus on what we are grateful for, the less space fear has to occupy us. We cannot feel fear while we are grateful. The next time you are feeling fearful or faced with anxiety, begin to focus on the good people in your life. The good things that people have done for you before, and the good things you have done for people.

This thinking will bring you back to a positive state of mind and drive away the fear or anxiety.

By remaining in this positive state, we are able to connect with others and leave them inspired. Then they will continue to spread that inspiration to others in their lives.

Choose to be as present and grateful as our dog friends.

Lifelong Learning and Discipline

I recently went to a showing of the movie Casablanca, brought to life by the Oregon Symphony. It was my first time watching the movie itself, and also the first time I had seen a movie with a live orchestra.

After the show, I was left with thoughts about the people in the orchestra. To be a part of the state symphony team, what an achievement!

Imagine the level of discipline required to reach that level. That is years of consistent learning and practice. That is a level of competition where one can never get complacent.

The moment you became complacent is the moment someone would take your seat.

It blew me away to put myself in their shoes. Getting that phone call from the person who decides who gets on the team and who does not and getting an invite. What a humbling and exciting experience that must be.

This is the reward for lifelong learning and discipline to your profession. The payoff of the sacrifices made in the pursuit of excellence, of being the best at what you do.

What is your lifelong pursuit?

Humility

I read a book once, named "An Astronaut's Guide to Life on Earth" by Colonel Chris Hadfield, the first Canadian astronaut to go to space.

In his book, Mr. Hadfield talks about how so many people try to be a plus one in life, when it is better to aim to be a zero. The other option is to be a negative one, which means you're taking away from other's life experience. By aiming to be a zero, you generally add to other's life experience.

He uses a reference of the types of astronauts who refuse to even push the button on an elevator for others. Those are the plus ones who think they're too good for such a thing.

The zeroes are the ones who, despite reaching high levels of status in life, retain enough humility to still push the button for others. They don't mind giving the credit to someone else, they're just happy the team is successful, and enjoy seeing others achieve.

I can't tell you how many times I have gone into a bathroom to see both paper towel and toilet paper all over the floor. It blows my mind every time I see it.

Can you imagine? Tossing a dirty paper towel toward the garbage can, it bounces off and falls on the floor, and you just walk out of the bathroom. That is some of the laziest stuff I've ever seen!

These are the "not my job" kind of people that skate by on bare minimum to get paid.

They are exercising the exact opposite of the wisdom that Napoleon Hill shared, "The man who does more than he is paid for will soon be paid more than he does."

You have to give value before you can receive. That is the golden rule in life.

So those people that just leave their garbage on the floor for others to pick up can be confident that they won't be receiving much from the universe. If you're a detriment to it, why in the world would it stick it's neck out to give you a hand? It won't.

People that lack humility are the same that use their title or position to force others to do their bidding, rather than use their language to influence others to rally behind a mission. They are the ones that garner little to no genuine respect. So as soon as those employees receive an offer that gives them more pay than what they're receiving now, they will jump ship and not look back.

And some "leaders" in business say that the younger generations have no loyalty. It is the leader's responsibility to set the standard. When those leaders lack humility, they will lack the loyalty of others.

Choose to retain your humility, no matter what your title or position is. You will likewise retain your ability to influence others to join you in your mission and bring it to fruition.

Sometimes There Are No Second Chances

There are situations in life where we only get one chance, no do-overs. Some opportunities are truly once in a lifetime.

Life is a beautiful journey, with real rewards and real risks.

Some of those risks could mean our very lives. Yes, this is a more serious chapter, one that is worth taking heed of.

In today's modern society, a majority of people are shielded from seeing the viciousness of mistakes or bad choices.

This is a friendly reminder to think twice before doing something that you know could put your life at stake. This includes robbing someone, having sex with someone's wife (or girlfriend), getting blacked out drunk, doing hard drugs, and driving like an asshole where you shouldn't be.

We are blessed to live in a time where we can live many decades full of great experiences and making wonderful memories. Don't cut it short by being foolish.

Don't Be in Such a Hurry to Arrive to The Destination

Immediate gratification culture has done us a lot of damage for various reasons. One of these reasons is that we are always in a hurry to get "there."

Alan Watts had a wonderful way of looking at this.

"In music, one doesn't make the end of the composition the point of the composition.

If that were so, the best conductors would be those who played fastest, and there would be composers who wrote only finales. People would go to concerts just to hear one crashing chord — because that's the end!

But we don't see that as something brought by our education into our everyday conduct.

We've got a system of schooling that gives a completely different impression. It's all graded and what we do is we put the child into the corridor of this grade system, with a kind of, "Come on kitty kitty kitty!" and now you go to kindergarten, you know, and that's a great thing because when you finish that you'll get into first grade. And then — Come on! — first grade leads to second grade, and so on, and then you get out of grade school. You go to high school and it's revving up — The thing is coming! — then you're gonna go to college, and by jove, then you get into graduate school, and when you're through with graduate school you go out and join the world.

Then you get into some racket where you're selling insurance, and they've got that quota to make and you're gonna make that, and all the time "the thing" is coming — It's coming, it's coming! — that great thing: the success you're working for.

Then when you wake up one day, about 40 years old, you say, "My God, I've arrived! I'm there!" And you don't feel very different from what you always felt. And there's a slight let down because you feel there was a hoax.

And there was a hoax. A dreadful hoax.

They made you miss everything. We thought of life by analogy with a journey, with a pilgrimage, which had a serious purpose at the end, and the thing was to get to that end: success, or whatever it is, or maybe heaven after you're dead.

But we missed the point the whole way along.

It was a musical thing, and you were supposed to sing, or dance, while the music was being played."

Things Happen for Us, Not to Us

One of my mentors, Ed Mylett, taught me that things happen for us, not to us. This is a huge distinction to grasp. This means that everything is happening for a reason, not just happening randomly and without meaning.

I had my first true test of putting this into practice during a 3-hour drive home. I was about 80 miles away from home and I needed to get some more fuel. I took an exit and was trailing a fully loaded semi with a trailer.

As we neared the T in the road, I saw that we didn't have a stop sign and the other ends of the T did have stop signs. Both the semi and I were turning left, and I glanced out my driver's side window for a moment, checking out the scenery of an unfamiliar area.

WHAM! I came to a sudden stop as I slammed into the back of the semi's trailer. My airbag didn't deploy as I wasn't going that fast. I threw my vehicle into park, and took my seatbelt off, preparing to get out an assess the damage. Then I realized I was still on the off ramp from the highway, buckled back up, and began to follow the semi.

The semi driver continued to drive longer than I thought he would, and I had a thought, "maybe he didn't even feel that."

He pulled into a truck stop and after he came to a stop, I got out and walked up to his cab. Surprised, he rolled down his window. I asked if he knew that I had hit the back of his trailer, and he didn't have a clue. He let me know the reason he had slammed on his brakes at the T was because a driver on our right had ran the stop sign. It was just a case of timing, as I was looking out the wrong window when the driver ran the stop sign.

He got out and followed me to the back, checking out the damage. Lucky for me, only his ICC bar was slightly bent inward, which he was able to mostly straighten out. He wasn't too stressed out about the situation, so we exchanged information and went on our ways.

I was curious if my vehicle would be able to continue the drive the 80 or so miles, so I investigated to see if it was leaking any fluids or if it smelled weird. Neither were present, so I decided to get fuel and try to make it home.

As I was pumping the fuel, I began to get upset with myself for making such a boneheaded mistake. I griped and complained about the money I was about to waste fixing my vehicle.

Then I heard Ed's voice, "Things happen for us, not to us."

It made me think as the fuel nozzle clicked, my tank full. I hung it up, and got into the driver's seat, and began making my way back to the highway.

"What was the reason this happened?" I asked myself.

For one obvious one, it was a lesson in staying present. I had allowed myself to become distracted, only for a moment, but sometimes all it takes is a moment.

Quick disclaimer, I'm human too. I had been seeing a lot of people driving aggressively lately, following people too closely, and in a nutshell, being assholes on the road.

While witnessing these events, I had allowed the thought, "Maybe if they would just crash one time, they would stop being assholes."

Reason number two, I had wished ill will upon another person. Someone wiser than their years told me, "When you curse someone else, the only person you are cursing is yourself." Here I was reaping what I sewed.

I thought about the fact that I had not rear ended another passenger vehicle, which would have been more of a headache. Another fact was that I was not injured.

The last reason didn't come to me until after I had finished at the body shop, leaving my vehicle. I got home, and had a thought, "Maybe I can help a lot of people avoid a similar situation by sharing my story."

So, I made a post on my social medias, sharing what had occurred. While typing up the post, I realized that I had done a good job about one thing, I had stayed a positive influence on the people I interacted with after the accident.

Despite the circumstances, I decided I would leave others touched, moved, or inspired, rather than in a negative energy state after interacting with me.

Another story I have to share comes from one of my old colleagues, Paul. Paul had a bad accident where he lost a portion of his leg, under the knee.

He was faced with a choice – Would he allow this event to define his life, or would he define the event? He chose to define the event. He told me, "Brian, I could either be a victim, or I could continue to live my life as I had before the accident. I could choose to use my situation as a way to inspire others with similar situations. I wanted to show them that even with this sort of injury, we can still create the lives we want to."

Ego

We often compare ourselves and our achievements against other people. The only thing that really matters though is how we compare to ourselves. Are we a better us than we were yesterday? Last year? Ten years ago?

When we are stuck in a pattern of comparing ourselves to others rather than ourselves, we are operating out of our ego. So, what if we're not as strong, intelligent, or "far along" as another person? They are living their life, and we are living our life.

In this life, it is us vs. us. That's it.

Our ego is what feeds us lies. It tells us, "You're not good enough." "You haven't pushed yourself hard enough today, you're lazy." "You think that other person thinks you're sexy? Hah! You might as well go eat another candy bar."

The ego also does the opposite. It will make us believe that we're incredible, better than another person, or that someone is lucky that we're in their lives.

Our ego is all about tripping us up. When we operate from our ego, we end up with bruised shins and stubbed toes. Sometimes even broken noses.

Not only does it cause us metaphorical (and sometimes literal) injury, it leaves us with an emptiness inside. When we levy judgement on another, what we are really doing is covering up our own self-loathing by making someone else smaller.

When we judge another, we are really just judging ourselves.

What good does it do us to walk around with judgement in our hearts? None.

At the end of the day, our judgement means nothing. We are not the Judge.

Does that mean we have to accept bad behavior from others? Absolutely not! When we love ourselves, we don't allow others to abuse us or walk over us. We can still love them though.

Our happiness is directly related to how much self-love we have for ourselves. I would argue that if we don't love ourselves, we cannot truly be happy.

If we do not love ourselves, we cannot love others. There will always be judgement in our heart. I believe we cannot even fully receive love from another. We will always put up a wall of some height or another, to limit the love we allow ourselves to receive from others.

When they tell us, "You look great today," our ego will tell us, *"They're just telling us that to help us feel better."* And you'll believe it.

What is the path to loving ourselves? We have to be brutally honest and tell the truth to ourselves. We have to forgive ourselves and we have to forgive others.

If we are harboring any resentment, guilt, or regret in our heart, we will be denied the self-love that we all long for.

Strap yourselves in, because we're about to get deep here for a moment.

Right now, you may be thinking to yourself, "Yeah, but he doesn't know what happened to me." Or, "Yeah, sure, easy to say, but my friend or family member went through this."

This especially applies in even the most dire of past traumas. Rape, for example.

In the past, someone raped another person. This actually did happen. There is no disputing that it did happen, because it did.

How long ago? Some people are living their lives ten, twenty, or even fifty years in the future after that even happened, as if it happened yesterday.

This next part is important to grasp. That event did not happen yesterday. After something has happened in our lives, it only exists in our mind. We create a story about the situation that happened, and we begin to tell ourselves lies.

We tell ourselves that we will never be whole again. We tell ourselves that asked for it. We tell ourselves that we are not worthy of love now because of what happened.

All lies. A story made up in our minds.

We have become so accustomed to the emotions and feelings we get from the story that we forget that we have the ability to let it go.

Whatever we practice repeatedly takes on a sort of muscle memory, even thoughts. At a certain point, we don't even have to try, the thoughts just surface on their own will. A sort of momentum forms that is self-propelling.

Depending on how much momentum there is, what I'm writing could really piss someone off, and cause them to even lash out at me.

The truth is that we are all deserving and worthy of self-love, receiving love from another person, and loving another person.

We must choose to forgive ourselves first. Whoever did this thing is responsible, we are not. Then we must forgive the person who did it. Which part of the two is harder, is different for each individual. Without forgiveness on both ends, there will always be a sort of wound that cannot heal. We can clean it every once in a while, but it will continue to bleed and become infected over time.

Forgiveness will cure the wound, allowing it to become a scar. We have the memory, but not the emotion that went along with it.

Many people go to therapy for years, sometimes even their entire lives, essentially placing a new band-aid over their wound, over and over again as they continue to fall off. I'm not saying therapy is a bad thing, or that therapists do not do good work and help people. What I am saying is that if we can forgive ourselves and forgive the other person, we will no longer need therapy.

Therapy is only needed when we have a wound.

Just like the goal of physical therapy is to get a person back to full functionality and strength, the goal of mental therapy is to get a person back to wholeness and self-love.

Choose to let go of the past. Forgive yourself, forgive the other person, and truly begin living into a new future you are creating for yourself. One not tethered by the past.

You matter. Your life matters.

The Beauty of Life

A sunset. A sunrise. The view from 14,000 feet flying over a mountain. Watching the waves of an ocean roll in. Flowers in bloom. A dog running after a ball with its tail wagging. Hearing and seeing a baby laugh.

Life is beautiful. There are so many opportunities throughout our days to see the beauty, but in today's fast-paced world it can be easy to forget that.

We have so much to be grateful for. We are a part of this beautiful world.

Instead of being hard on ourselves for our big ears, or being too short, or having a scar from an accident, or insert anything you wish was different about yourself, realize that you are perfect the way you are. Just to be alive proves that. Out of all the possibilities that could have occurred, you are what is here. In this universe there are actually no accidents, and neither are you.

You are perfect the way you are.

Perhaps there is nothing more beautiful from a human being than a laugh or a smile. Challenge yourself to help three people laugh or smile today.

Assets

Monopoly was truly a great lesson in what should be a major objective for us in life – accumulating assets.

Until we build a portfolio of assets that generate us revenue without us having to trade our time for money, we will always need to work. Always trading time for money.

Wouldn't it be great to wake up on the first of the month, check your bank account, and see a deposit of $30,000.00 every month from your rental properties? Or to get a phone call from one of your trusted investment advisors after new year's, letting you know that your investment portfolio with them had a record-smashing year and you earned 12% on your portfolio for the previous year?

It only takes two things to realize this reality for yourself. It takes getting started and discipline.

In all things consistency is king, and investing is no exception. The mistake many make is thinking that they're still young and can afford to wait. The truth couldn't be farther from that. It is only when some people reach their 40's, or even 50's, when that truth smacks them in the face, and they realize they made a terrible mistake.

At some point in our lives, sooner for some, later for others, it will become more difficult to trade time for money. Our bodies generally age faster than our minds do, and we overestimate what we may be capable of doing.

No disrespect meant, but this is why there are greeters at Walmart. Do you think for a second any of those individuals envisioned a life in their late years standing at the doors of Walmart to say hello to people? Not a chance.

There are many reasons that people will tell you that they're in this situation, but the stone-cold truth of the matter is they didn't prepare well enough. That is all there is to it.

This fate is completely avoidable. It takes disciple and it takes sacrifice. Choose and commit to not finding yourself at the sliding doors of Walmart in your senior years.

Your future self will be grateful that your younger self had the willpower to stay the course to avoid that reality.

So the next time you are thinking about blowing your commitment to your budget, and think you will just catch up next paycheck, really stop and picture yourself standing there saying hello to people as they walk in. Really take the time to envision this future, and you will have a good chance at resisting the instant gratification that you're considering trading for that future.

Water or Wine?

Disclaimer – this is not an indictment on anyone. I'm far from a perfect human being. I enjoy having an old fashioned or glass of merlot like many do.

With that out of the way, there is nothing on the planet that causes more heartache and loss than alcohol.

I couldn't count the number of people I have met personally as well as seen share their story online that have acknowledged that without alcohol in their lives, they wouldn't have hit rock bottom.

There are those that have killed other people while driving drunk. There are those that have developed cirrhosis of the liver, heart disease, and cancer as a result of overconsumption. There is the abusive parent or spouse that beats their children and significant other.

Alcohol is one of those things in life where it can easily become too much of a good thing, fast.

One of the reasons for this is because in many parts of the world, particularly in the U.S., there is a massive party culture. And alcohol is the legal, socially accepted option.

A major issue with this is that it does not only affect the people who choose to partake. Similar to cigarettes, alcohol affects those in proximity or those that come in contact with people who have been drinking. It isn't an isolated impact.

I had a cousin that decided to be responsible one New Year's Eve, where he offered to be a designated driver for his friends. On the drive to drop everyone off, a drunk driver went over the center line on the highway, hitting my cousin's car, and my cousin's car was knocked off the highway into a pole.

Out of everyone in the car, my cousin was the only person to die. This happens quite often, where the only person who doesn't survive a drinking and driving accident is the person who has not been drinking.

Even in a world where we can hail a cost-effective Uber or Lyft, people still choose to drive after they have been drinking. It is one of the strangest things to me.

Drinking can be fun and enjoyable in the right context and in the right amounts. It is one of the crutches that people lean too heavily on too often to combat their own social anxiety and low self-esteem or self-confidence.

It is interesting to go on a night out without drinking when most people are drinking. I have not personally experienced more peer pressure than when I do this.

People will say, "You can have just one drink, no big deal." "Come on, just have one." "What, are you an alcoholic?" "You will have more fun if you just have a drink."

It is quite comical, really. Anytime someone feels the urge to say something like this, it is because they could not imagine being out without drinking themselves. So instead of facing that fact, they attempt to bring a person who has the inner confidence and willpower to be out sober to their level so they will drink with them.

Drink responsibly is a great phrase, but too often we go beyond that.

Another great phrase is, do you, don't pressure others to be like you.

Who Succeeds?

By Earl Nightingale:

"The only man who succeeds is the man who is progressively realizing a worthy ideal. He is the man who says, "I am going to become this," and then begins to work towards that goal.

I'll tell you who the successful people are. The success is the school teacher who is teaching school because that's what he wanted to do.

The success is the woman who is a wife and mother because she wanted to become a wife and mother and is doing a good job of it.

The success is the man who runs the corner gas station because that's what he wanted to do.

The success is the successful salesman who wants to become a top-notch salesman and grow and build with his organization.

A success is anyone who is doing deliberately a pre-determined job because that's what he decided to do deliberately. But only 1 out of 20 does that. That's why today there isn't really any competition unless we make it for ourselves.

Instead of competing, all we have to do is create.

Now for 20 years, I looked for the key which would determine what would happen to a human being. Was there a key, I wanted to know, which would make the future a promise that we could foretell to a large extent?

WAS THERE A KEY THAT WOULD GUARANTEE A PERSON'S BECOMING SUCCESSFUL IF HE ONLY KNEW ABOUT IT AND KNEW HOW TO USE IT?

Well, there is such a key. And I found it.

Here is the key to success and the key to failure. We become what we think about.

Now let me say that again. We become what we think about."

It was Napoleon Hill that said, "Thoughts are things."

Our Time Together Comes to an End, For Now – Before We Go, Legacy

As I mentioned earlier, it would be an oxymoron if this book was too long.

I do not live with many regrets, but one of the few regrets this author does have is not using my natural gifts sooner in my life. Two of my biggest gifts are my baseline emotions of enthusiasm and positivity, and writing.

The emotions have helped greatly in my sales career – they have allowed me to consistently improve in my ability to deliver maximum value outcomes for the clients that I serve. Sales is probably the profession that is filled with the most rejection and takes a certain type of DNA to do for a living. You have to know that the company and solutions you represent are the best for the people you are working with and could potentially work with. My baseline emotions allow me to bounce back from rejection and focus instead on the belief that I am the best strategic partner for the people I work with.

Where I've neglected this gift is in my ambition and application. Or put another way, how much of a scope I've had in sharing them with the world. Now, I am committed to continual improvement in every area and aspect that I can, with as many people as I can. I know my energy and belief is contagious, and I have a duty to share that with people that need it. Belief leads to achievement, and achievement leads to fulfillment.

The second is my writing – I have been one of those people for too long, that knew they had a talent, but didn't actively deploy it. No longer – this ability was gifted to me for a reason, and that reason is it is meant to be shared with the world.

What are your gifts? You know them in your heart. You have probably heard people throughout your life tell you exactly what your gifts are. Which, by the way, people that realize someone's gifts and then shares with them those gifts are the best leaders on the planet. They create undefeatable levels of belief in a person, that can put them on a course in their life that leads them to the greatest version of themselves.

And that leads me to legacy:

We all must choose what type of, and how big of an impact we will make in the world while we are here. It can be big, or it can be small. It can help change millions of lives, or it can help change a handful of lives. Both are good, but why not go big?

Bonus Rule

Fulfillment = Leveraging our gifts + helping as many people as we can with them

Zig Ziglar was right on the money when he said, "You can get everything in life you want if you will just help enough other people get what they want."

Don't settle for mediocrity, walk toward greatness on a daily basis.

Acknowledgements

Throughout my life there have been many people who have helped me at critical moments, and plenty of times where someone gave me a friendly smile in passing when I needed it. This is by no means a complete or exhaustive list of "thank you's" owed.

My grandmother – Without my grandma's influence on me, I wouldn't be half the person I am today. She taught me humility, kindness, and patience. If it wasn't for her, I don't know if I would like to read, and without that, I surely wouldn't have ever written this book.

My father – Without my dad changing our family's course and breaking our curse, where father and son did not share emotions with one another, it would have been more difficult to break our paycheck to paycheck curse. He passed the torch to me, and now it is my turn to be the one who creates generational wealth for my family.

My aunts and uncles – I have two sets of aunts and uncles that really stepped up to the plate for me in a big way. I'll spare everyone the juicy details here, but needless to say, they showed up when I needed them.

My cousin – More like a sister to me than a cousin. We grew up together, and most recently I have seen her turn into a great mother to her son. So proud of you, cuz.

My mother – Life is full of learning and growing, and you've done a lot of that. You've been a role model for me in growth and change.

My friends – I know it is rare to have friends from childhood that are actually positive influences on you. I have met so many people in my life that have helped shape my perspective and belief – there have been times I would have failed without my friends.

The bosses, managers, leaders I've worked for and the colleagues I've worked with – Living in four states, I have had a wide variety of each in my lifetime. I know the value of people-focused, future-focused, and growth-focused leadership, and have experienced when there is a void. I'm grateful for those people that took their roles as leaders seriously.

The organizations I've worked for – Whether it was fast food, retail, a video rental store, manufacturing, a gas station, UPS overnight, assembly line work, or sales – every one of the companies I have worked for has led to me becoming the professional I am today. Thank you for the growth opportunities you provided.

Andy Frisella and Ed Mylett – Between your podcasts, keynote speeches, and creating Arete, you guys have helped me more than anyone when it comes to discipline, perspective, belief, business, and personal growth.

Arete – We will change the world together by changing the entrepreneurial and business space.

God – Without you, nothing is possible. Every day I have to share my enthusiasm and belief with others is a blessing, and I'm grateful to you for that. There have been so many times in my life where I can't explain it any other way.

Example One

One night, I was walking home at 1am from my night shift. I was walking through snow halfway up my shins along the highway, because I grew up in in the Midwest, and had no car when I was 16. Suddenly, the word *duck* came to my mind, and I did. A whizzing sound went passed me, where my head had just been a moment before. I inspected what the object was in the deep snow, and discovered it was a frozen water bottle.

I would have probably died in that snow had that bottle hit me.

Example Two

During a baseball game, the batter cracked a really high pop fly over the fence, right for where I was sitting with a girl I went to the game with. As I watched it sail, my adrenaline came flooding out of the gates when I realized that ball was headed straight toward us. Her, to be specific. She wasn't even paying attention as this ball was zooming toward her head. A strange calm washed over me, and I reached out at the last moment, catching the ball with upturned palm. Boy did that sting bad. I am good, but I defer to having had help on that catch and avoiding the catastrophe that could have been.

Example Three

I have survived a head-on car accident where the vehicles were going 30/55 mph. (with seat belt on) – My friend who was riding shotgun also walked away with nothing outside of a scar on his face, which would surprise you if you saw a picture of my car. The front end had come in so far my friend's legs were shoved back into his chest at a weird angle. The other driver who wasn't wearing his seat was also okay, outside of the broken ribs from slamming into the steering wheel that snapped in half.

And the baby in the other car was also perfectly OK.

Thank you, God.

www.ingramcontent.com/pod-product-compliance
Lightning Source LLC
Chambersburg PA
CBHW031628040426
42452CB00007B/726